CU00983898

THE MIND IN THE HEART
Michael Ramsey: Theologian and Man of Prayer

LORNA KENDALL

SLG Press
Convent of the Incarnation
Fairacres Oxford

ISBN 0 7283 0130 X
ISSN 0307-1405

ACKNOWLEDGEMENT

The quotation on page 4, from Jesus and the Living Past,
is used by permission of Oxford University Press.

*This study of Michael Ramsey originated in a paper given in Canterbury
to the group 'Groundwork for a Lay Theology', on 22 November 1989,
and to The Anselm Society, on 11 October 1990.*

I FIRST KNEW MICHAEL RAMSEY when I was an undergraduate at Cambridge and he was the young unmarried vicar of St Benet's who was often to be seen browsing in the book shops or, like everybody else, pedalling round the streets on his old bicycle. He had recently come to Cambridge from being sub-Warden of Lincoln Theological College where, at the age of thirty-two, he had written his first, and perhaps most influential, book, *The Gospel and the Catholic Church*,[1] a book which half a century later is still an important book for theological students and ordinands. As Gordon Wakefield has written,

> It established him as a mature theologian and, together with his personality and presence, inspired a certain awe in pupils and colleagues alike, an awe which remained, though he was the humblest of archbishops, to the end.[2]

It is said that this sense of awe sometimes distanced Ramsey from his clergy, who at diocesan gatherings or vicarage meals seemed to be intimidated by what they took to be the Archbishop's awkward silences. Not so the students at Lincoln, of whom it is said that some of them once took a bet as to which of them, when they went to get back their essays, would prolong their young tutor's silence the longest! I used to wonder whether some of the clergy felt ill at ease because they themselves read little. Conversation always flowed if the Archbishop were asked, 'What are you reading?', or 'What ought I to be reading?'

He sometimes showed great enthusiasm for a particular book which he tended to carry round with him to show to others in the hope they would share his enthusiasm and pass it on. One such example, I remember, was Léon-Dufour's book on the Gospels when it came into an English edition in 1968.[3] The main reason for his excitement—and this is not too strong a word—is that in this book Ramsey saw clear evidence that Roman Catholic scholars were taking the findings of biblical criticism seriously and were writing books that could be read and understood by intelligent lay people as well as by priests

1

and professional theologians.

Like all great teachers, Ramsey remained an enthusiastic student to the end of his life. Perhaps it was for this reason that he kept his sense of fun, and often irrepressible laughter, to the end. He once remarked to me in fun that his favourite book was *A Canterbury Pewside Book*, a book of humorous cartoons and photographs illustrating the many facets of his life in Church and State when he was Archbishop of Canterbury. As a theologian he was never overbearing or portentous, and all who were privileged to glimpse his radiant spirituality knew that it was never artificial, pompous or intense. It seems right to begin an appraisal of Michael Ramsey as a theologian and man of prayer with some recollection of his character.

Early Career

Although we now have Professor Owen Chadwick's authorized biography, *Michael Ramsey: A Life,*[4] perhaps a few biographical details, especially in relation to his academic career, may be helpful.

Ramsey felt himself to be overshadowed during his youth by his outstandingly brilliant elder brother, Frank, who was to die in early manhood. But when Ramsey went up to Magdalene College, Cambridge, the academic excellence already in evidence at Repton manifested itself. In his first term he won the Latin Verse Prize. His remarkable versatility and force as a debater won him a place in a four-man team which toured the United States in the Summer vacation of 1925, and in 1926, the distinction of becoming President of the Cambridge Union. His interests and abilities suggested that he would have had a brilliant career in law or politics or government, but with the dawning of a strong sense of vocation he changed course. After taking a First in the Theological Tripos he proceeded in 1927 to Cuddesdon Theological College to prepare for ordination.

Although Sir Edwyn Hoskyns was not Ramsey's tutor at Cambridge before his untimely death in 1937, he made a great impression on Ramsey during his undergraduate days. In the article in *Theology* Gordon Wakefield analyses in some detail those characteristics of Ramsey's theology which, in his view, are clearly due to Hoskyns's influence. Here I wish to emphasize one particular passage in Ramsey's own writing where he acknowledges his indebtedness to Hoskyns, a passage which is worth quoting at some length, both because it records the profound effect of Hoskyns on Cambridge theological scholarship at that time, and also because it illustrates his deep and lasting influence on Ramsey the theologian. Ramsey's book, *The Resurrection of Christ,* opens this way:

> The writer of this book remembers receiving something of a shock when it was first his privilege to attend the lectures of the late Sir Edwyn Hoskyns. The lecturer began with the declaration that as our subject was the Theology and Ethics of the New Testament we must begin with the passages about the Resurrection. It seemed to contradict all the obvious preconceptions. Was it not right to trace first the beginnings of the ministry of Jesus, the events of His life and the words of His teaching? Here, surely, the essence of the Gospel might be found, and as a finale the Resurrection comes so as to seal and confirm the message. No. The Resurrection is a true starting-place for the study of the making and the meaning of the New Testament.[5]

This was the conviction underlying *The Gospel and the Catholic Church.* In this book, written at an age when most Anglican clergymen have barely completed their post-ordination training, Ramsey examined the meaning of the Christian Church in relation to the Death and Resurrection of Jesus. In this, as in all his later books, he was able to distil a vast background of scholarship into lucid prose, using the technical terms of academic theology (as in the exegesis of biblical words and phrases) only when no other would do. In the first part of the book he develops his thesis that

> The study of the New Testament points to the Death and Resurrection of the Messiah as the central theme of the Gospels and Epistles, and shows that these events were intelligible only to those who shared in them by a more than metaphorical dying and rising again with Christ. It is the contention of this book that in His dying and rising again the very meaning of the Church is found and that the Church's outward order expresses its inward meaning by representing the dependence of the members upon the one Body, wherein they die to self. The doctrine of the Church is thus found to be included within the Christian's knowledge of Christ crucified.[6]

Throughout a long life Ramsey retained an interest in current theological debate, and he was ever ready to defend his early thesis, clear and axiomatic in the main argument of *The Gospel and the Catholic Church*, that historically the Gospel precedes the Church. Thus in his last book but one, written in his retirement, he takes issue with Protestant scholars like John Knox (the twentieth century one!) who argue that, because there is no knowledge of Jesus apart from the Church, the historical event of Christ is indistinguishable from the coming into existence of the Church. Michael Ramsey wrote:

> While it is from the Church alone that we know about Jesus, the Church existed in utter dependence upon a Jesus who had existed before it and had created it. The language of St Paul affirms the utter dependence upon Jesus of the apostles and the Christian community.
> . . . We need not hesitate to say that the event of Jesus is distinguishable from the event of the Church.[7]

In *The Gospel and the Catholic Church* we see the first flowering of Ramsey's life-long interest in, and dedication to, the work of Christian unity and the reunion of Christendom. In the first instance this stemmed from his own family background and experience. His father, Arthur Stanley Ramsey, was a devout Congregationalist so it was not until he was at school at Repton that Michael presented himself for confirmation in the Church of England. His concern for Christian unity stemmed in the second instance from deeply rooted theological convictions. A large part of *The Gospel and the Catholic Church* is taken up with a detailed study of Christian history in East and West, in Catholicism, Eastern Orthodoxy, Protestantism and Anglicanism, all in relation to those facts about the Gospel and the Church which he believed the study of origins had disclosed. So he came to a conclusion which he spent the next fifty years working out in precept, prayer and practice. He wrote in 1936:

> . . . as the débris of old controversies and one-sided systems is cleared away, there appears the pattern of a structure, whose maker and builder is God.
>   The return of all Christians to this divine structure is not a movement backwards to something ancient and venerable, nor a submission on the part of some to what especially belongs to others. It is the recognition by all of the truth about themselves as members of the one people of God, whose origin is the historical life of Jesus and

4

whose completeness will be known only in the building up of the one Body. For every part of Christendom this recognition means not only the recovery of the one Church order, but the experience of the Passion of Jesus wherein that order has its meaning. Hence the movement towards reunion consists not only or even primarily in the discussions between churches or in their schemes of readjustment, imperative though these may be. It consists rather in the growth within every part of the Church of the truths of the Body and the Passion, no less than of the ' outward marks ' which express those truths. The unification of outer order can never move faster than the recovery of inward life. . . . No Christian shall deny his Christian experience, but all Christians shall grow more fully into the one experience in all its parts.[8]

Years later, when Michael Ramsey was Archbishop of York, during a Week of Prayer for Christian Unity he ended a sermon in Birmingham Cathedral with these words:

I pray that we may not seek the domination of one denomination over another; but the domination of the Gospel over us all.

Durham to Canterbury

So great was the impact of *The Gospel and the Catholic Church*, that in 1939, during the war and despite his youth, Michael Ramsey was appointed Canon of Durham Cathedral and Van Mildert Professor of Divinity in the University where he spent ten happy years exerting great leadership in reshaping the Faculty with a team of distinguished colleagues.

In one of his *Cambridge Sermons*, Sir Edwyn Hoskyns had asked the students:

Can we rescue a word, and discover a universe? Can we study a language, and awake to the Truth? Can we bury ourselves in a lexicon, and arise in the presence of God?[9]

Michael Ramsey could always do that, and one such word, perhaps his favourite, was the word *glory*. It was in Durham that Professor Ramsey wrote *The Glory of God and the Transfiguration of Christ*,[10] and these words of Hoskyns preceded the Table of Contents. It is a book which demonstrates Ramsey's power of biblical exegesis at its best, starting as it does with an examination of the concept of glory and the language used to describe it in the Old Testament.

5

Nowhere are the tensions of Biblical theology greater than in the doctrine of the glory. It speaks on the one hand of an invisible and omnipresent God and on the the other hand of a meteorological phenomenon; on the one hand of Israel's transcendent king and judge and on the other hand of a presence tabernacling in Israel's midst. But in these tensions the validity of the theology of the Old Testament lies. 'Am I a God at hand, saith the LORD, and not a God afar off?' (Jer. xiii, 23). Always in tension these contrasted aspects of the divine glory find their true unity when the Word by whom all things were made became flesh and dwelt among us, and the glory of Bethlehem and Calvary is the glory of the eternal God.[11]

The rest of the book examines the Transfiguration of Christ in the New Testament and in the Church. He understands the significance of the Transfiguration of Christ not only for the Church but also for the world thus:

[The Transfiguration] stands as a gateway to the saving events of the Gospel, and is as a mirror in which the Christian mystery is seen in its unity.

Confronted as he is with a universe more than ever terrible in the blindness of its processes and the destructiveness of its potentialities mankind must be led to the Christian faith not as a panacea of progress nor as an other-worldly solution unrelated to history, but as a Gospel of Transfiguration. Such a Gospel both transcends the world and speaks to the immediate here-and-now. He who is transfigured is the Son of Man; and, as He discloses on mount Hermon another world, He reveals that no part of created things and no moment of created time lies outside the power of the Spirit, who is Lord, to change from glory to glory.[12]

In 1950 Ramsey moved from Durham to the prestigious Regius Professorship in Cambridge. Students flocked to his lectures, but hardly had he established himself once more in Cambridge than the call came to return to Durham as Bishop. So back to this well-loved place he went in 1952. He was only forty-seven. This was the end of his career as a professional theologian; if he regretted it, he rarely, if ever, admitted it, although Gordon Wakefield suggested that 'There was more than a little wistfulness in his Lewis Carroll reference, when he responded on behalf of the honorary graduands at London University: "I was a real turtle once." '[13]

Nevertheless, Ramsey's links with university life were never severed and always gave him much pleasure. One of his great enjoyments continued to be 'off the cuff' question and answer sessions with students whenever these could be arranged. By the time of his death he had received approximately thirty honorary doctorates in theology from universities all over the world. He was in constant demand to give single lectures to university audiences. For example, in 1962 he addressed the University of Athens on 'Constantinople and Canterbury', and in 1963 the University of London on 'Christianity and the Supernatural'. Both these lectures were delivered after he became Archbishop of Canterbury.

It is said that when he went to Rome to hold discussions with Pope Paul VI, Archbishop Ramsey did not need a retinue of advisers to compose theological answers for him. He was always ready to give them himself. Ramsey's own love of theology made him ready to encourage theological study on however small a scale. He found it strange that Canterbury had no forum for theological debate. So, as soon as Christ Church College and the University were established, he founded a small theological society which he named The Anselm Society in honour of his great predecessor. He took a keen interest in it, was its first president, and, whenever he could find time, read a paper to it. The Society is still in existence, and has held well over a hundred meetings.

After only four years as Bishop of Durham, and in line with other great scholar-Bishops of Durham of the ancient and recent past, Michael Ramsey became Archbishop of York in 1956. Whilst Archbishop of York he found time to make a significant contribution to academic scholarship. This time it was in the field of historical theology. He was invited to give the Hale Memorial Lectures at Seabury Western Theological Seminary in the United States in 1959. They were entitled *From Gore to Temple*,[14] their purpose being to trace the development of Anglican theology from 1889 to 1939, from the publication of *Lux Mundi* to the outbreak of the Second World War.

To begin with Gore and to end with Temple was in itself an opportunity to expound the thought of two very great scholar-Bishops who exerted a great influence in their time. Ramsey

7

was under no illusions as to the magnitude of the limitations of the task he set himself. In the Epilogue to the lectures he stated:

> The sketch of an era of Anglican theology is now ended. Among the hazards in the writing of it, none has been greater than that of describing Anglican thought apart from the story of Christian thought in its widest setting. The task has been possible only because Anglican theology in this era had a certain isolation.[15]

Whose Prayer is True

Michael Ramsey moved to Canterbury as Archbishop in 1961, remaining there until 1974, the longest time he spent in any one post. Called to leadership in a church which attributes great importance to the lives and writings of the early Fathers of the Church, it is appropriate to draw attention to the fact that he was a theologian in the ancient sense of the word of 'one whose prayer is true'. For him there was never any dichotomy, any false separation, between theology and prayer. His study of the Bible was the well-spring of his personal prayer and the source of his refreshment of spirit amid the burdens of church administration and ecclesiastical debate. His chaplains used to say that they often lost the Archbishop, whether at Lambeth or the Old Palace, but that he could usually be found quite quickly either in the library or the chapel.

It was a cause of sadness to him, as well as bewilderment, if clergy or ordinands found study wearisome. For him the study of Christian doctrine was never cold or barren and fed his pastoral life. In his inaugural address to the International Congress on Biblical Studies at Oxford in 1973, he began:

> It is with much diffidence that I address this Congress of learned students of the New Testament as it is now more than twenty years since I left the field of academic study and entered the hazardous life of what is called a church leader. However, I accepted the invitation to give this lecture in the belief that for the understanding of the gospel of Jesus Christ and its presentation in any phase of history, the role of the historian or theologian is never wholly separate from the role of the pastor and the evangelist.[16]

Doctrine was vibrant with life because it spoke to him of the living Lord, and he encouraged his clergy to think of the articles of the Creed in this way.

> Do not treat the doctrines of the Creed as a string of impersonal items, like a row of bricks picked out of a box. Treat them as doctrines of Christ, as so many aspects of the mystery of which he is the centre. Thus the Father Almighty declares his almighty power most chiefly in showing mercy and pity—in the mercy and pity of Christ's Incarnation. Again, the Holy Catholic Church is Christ's family, Christ's household. The Communion of Saints is the company of those who reflect Christ's glory, and heaven is the enjoyment of Christ's radiance. See Christian doctrine in this way, and it will make all the difference to your study of it. . . . Think of study rather as being refreshed from the deep, sparkling well of truth which is Christ himself.[17]

I once asked Ramsey, 'Who of all your ninety-nine predecessors on the chair of St Augustine do you think was the greatest?' Without a moment's hesitation he replied, 'St Anselm.' St Anselm was Archbishop of Canterbury 1093–1109. Ramsey, like Anselm in his great *Proslogion*, and in the tradition of the early Fathers, was one who 'made his theology a prayer'.[18] Nowhere is this more apparent than in his meditations on the Passion in St John's Gospel, given on many occasions. In the following commentary on the narrative of the Foot-washing (John 13:1–16), the keyword is again *glory*:

> Notice the words with which the evangelist introduces the feet-washing scene. 'Jesus, knowing that the Father had given all things into his hands, and that he had come from God and was going to God . . . ' He washed their feet as one to whom divine authority completely belonged. He is showing to the disciples and to us what the divine glory is really like.
> What is the glory of God really like? The glory of the infinite and eternal God who rules and sustains the universe? Men had longed to know. Now the veil is drawn aside: the glory of God is like Jesus washing the feet of the disciples. It is the glory of a God who humbles himself. Think how God humbles himself in his relations to the world, in the humble birth in the manger at Bethelehem, in Calvary, in all his gentle and patient dealings with ourselves. In that humility of God we see what the glory of God is like.
> Our worship means humbling ourselves before the God who is himself humble.[19]

For Ramsey theology, prayer and the practice of the Christian life were all interlocking parts of one whole. There is a famous prayer in St Anselm's *Proslogion* which ends with these words, words which could well be applied to Michael Ramsey:

> I do not seek to understand so that I may believe,
> but I believe so that I may understand;
> and what is more,
> I believe that unless I do believe I shall not understand.[20]

John Robinson's *Honest to God* was published in 1963 soon after Ramsey became Archbishop of Canterbury. Perhaps because it appeared to him to invert this relationship of faith and understanding and to strike a blow against traditional theology and spirituality, he over-reacted and uncharacteristically rushed into print. Almost at once, amid all the duties of his position, the Archbishop began to explore and to grasp what he later called 'the contemporary gropings and quests which lay behind *Honest to God*,' and confessed to having been 'a learner amidst the changing and unpredictable scenes of the 1960's'.[21] As a consequence he wrote two books dealing with contemporary theological trends, *Sacred and Secular*, the Holland Lectures for 1964, and *God, Christ and the World: A Study in Contemporary Theology*, in 1969. It is in the realms of prayer, and of contemplative prayer in particular, that he sees the balance held between the this-worldly and the other-worldly strands in the life of the Christian community. He lays particular emphasis on the view that contemplation

> concerns not only theology but the practical Christianity of every day. Whereas mental meditation is something in which not every Christian will persevere because the powers of the human mind in concentration and imagination vary so greatly, the contemplation of God with the ground of the soul is, as these old writers insisted, accessible to any man, woman or child who is ready to try to be obedient and humble and to want God very much.[22]

Not only on account of his own deep humility, but also because he recognized in John Robinson a fellow theologian 'whose prayer was true' he was prepared to support Bishop Robinson's appointment as Dean of Trinity College, Cambridge, and to write to him in these terms:

> I feel full of thankfulness for your 'Woolwich' time—in what you have

given to so many, both clergy and others, in your shepherding of them so lovingly, in what you have given to us in the central discussions of our church, and in your pioneering in the theological tasks before us.

I reproach myself with having been rather 'slow' in understanding, but I have found myself increasingly learning from you and increasingly being grateful.

I enclose my latest little—very little book [*God, Christ and the World*] —as a tiny mark of love and thankfulness.[23]

Quotations such as I have given from *Sacred and Secular* on contemplative prayer indicate that Michael Ramsey was a teacher of prayer as well as a master of prayer. Almost everything he wrote is shot through with the importance of prayer and worship (apparent if not always explicit). This is evident in his first book, *The Gospel and the Catholic Church*, published in 1936, which has a remarkable chapter on worship. He demonstrates in the light of New Testament insights, that Christian prayer is in essence neither mystical nor prophetical, but liturgical. And it is still evident in his last book *Be Still and Know*, published in 1982, which is a distillation of his teaching on prayer in the New Testament and in Christian life. There is recurrent emphasis on his conviction 'that stillness and silence are of supreme importance and that the neglect of them is damaging to the Christian life.'[24] A few months before he died he told me that *Be Still and Know* had sold better than all his other books. That seemed to give him quiet satisfaction.

Deep Things Simply

During his long and fruitful ministry thousands of confirmation candidates, ordinands, students, penitents, clergy and parishioners, as well as readers of his books, were grateful for and nourished by Ramsey's teaching, prayer and pastoral care. They often marvelled at his outstanding ability to combine clarity and simplicity with theological profundity. He used to say, 'If you can't express the deep things of the Faith simply you haven't understood them.' Only a few characteristic examples of his teaching on prayer can be added to those already given. He often used to meditate on the the prayer of Jesus and draw inspiration for Christian prayer. For example:

From our glimpse of Jesus praying on the hills of Galilee and in the

11

Garden of Gethsemane we pass to a familiar sight, the Christian who prays today.

To be with God for a space. . . . To be with God wondering, that is adoration. To be with God gratefully, that is thanksgiving. To be with God ashamed, that is contrition. To be with God with others on the heart, that is intercession. The secret is the quest of God's presence: 'Thy face Lord will I seek.' We shall indeed give forethought to the ways in which the time will be spent, but the outcome may be determined not only by our designs but by God's act in shaping both the time and ourselves. Thus our prayer is not only our own action but a divine energy with us as the Spirit within us cries, '*Abba*, Father.'[25]

So important is the Holy Spirit in the life of the Church and the spiritual life of the individual Christian that in 1977 Bishop Michael, as he preferred to be known in his retirement, wrote a book on this subject. Provost David Edwards, reviewing it in *The Church Times*, described it as being 'from the borderlands between doctrine and prayer'. Its significance for the life of prayer may be glimpsed from its concluding paragraph:

But it is a costly thing to invoke the Spirit, for the glory of Calvary was the cost of the Spirit's mission and is the cost of the Spirit's renewal. It is in the shadow of the cross that in any age of history Christians pray: Come, thou holy Paraclete.[26]

Intercessory prayer is at the heart of the prayer of Jesus who ever lives to make intercession for us (cf. Heb. 7:25b). In union with him intercession is at the heart of the priestly life and at the heart of the prayer of all Christians.

To intercede is to bear others on the heart in God's presence. Our own wantings have their place, for it is clear from the teaching of Jesus that God wants us to want and to tell him of our wants. When however we do this 'in the name of Jesus' we learn to bend our wantings to our glimpses of the divine will. Intercession thus becomes not the bombardment of God with requests so much as the bringing of our desires within the stream of God's own compassion.[27]

To hear Bishop Michael speak about prayer (or anything else) brought an added dimension of richness, either because he could say what he might not write, or because the smile in the eyes and raising of the legendary eyebrows accompanied his irrepressible sense of humour, even about serious things. For instance, during a School of Prayer which he gave in 1980 at St

Katharine's Foundation, Stepney, he said, 'God's compassion can sometimes be seen working through judgement. It may be the design of God for a statesman to become a perfect ass so that he might be got rid of!' Perhaps the statement still has topical relevance.

The Mind in the Heart

In a personal ecumenical message to Christians in France, Ramsey wrote that 'the study of truth and the lifting of the soul to God in prayer go together.' For him they always did. There would be something lacking, if not incongruous, if I spoke of Michael Ramsey only as a theologian and man of prayer without attempting to state how his scholarship and prayer related to the totality of his life and its responsibilities.

Ramsey was not called to study, write and pray alongside any of the Anglican monks whom he loved and admired, but to bear the burdens and responsibilities of high office for nearly a quarter of a century. The sheer weight of work should never be underestimated, nor the continual support that he received from his wife Joan, and the prayer of Anglican religious communities—the contemplative ones in particular, which he called his 'bolsters'. The cohesion of his life and work lies not in a resolution of the balance—if not conflict—between the active and contemplative which has been such a preoccupation of Western ascetic theology down the centuries, but rather in the fact that, steeped as he was in the traditions of the Eastern Orthodox Churches, he seemed to epitomize in his own life a precept of one of the Eastern Monks, 'Put thy mind into thy heart, and stand in the presence of God all day long.'

Another reason for the cohesion of the many activities of his life was the fact that he loved not only ideas but people, although his intense shyness sometimes prevented them from realizing this. As Archbishop and Primate he had to deal with many problems on a personal, national and international scale, and to write and speak about them. Whether he was dealing with the social problems arising from unemployment in the North of England (and he cared for Jarrow for this reason, as well as because it was the home of the Venerable Bede); or with the racial problems of South Africa; or with political injustice in

Rhodesia—as it then was; or with poverty in South America, behind his quick and penetrating grasp of the issues lay his pastoral concern and prayer for the people affected by them, his compassion for the world's need, and a theology which refused to be blinkered by what he used to call 'the domination of the contemporary', so that he could write:

> . . . we are called as Christians to a faith which both cares intensely about this world and is also set upon another world beyond it. The first is an immediate test of our Christianity. . . . Our concern in action for the hungry and homeless, for right dealing between different races, for the laws of conduct which God has given us, shows whether we love God whom we have not seen by the test of our love for the Brother we have seen. But as we serve this world and its needs we are all the while laying hold of something beyond this world, an eternal life which gives this world its true perspective. Let not that be forgotten.[28]

Retirement

When retirement came in 1974 many hoped that Bishop Michael would write a large book. He did not. For the last fifteen years of his life he emerged predominantly as a man and master of prayer. He lived very quietly at home most of the time, especially after the doctor told him that he must not travel by air, although he did travel abroad occasionally and was several times in residence at Nashotah House, Wisconsin, where he lectured on systematic theology and spirituality.

As it had been throughout his life, during these last years the very centre and mainspring of his life was the daily Office, and the daily Eucharist (and what a deprivation it was to him when he could not be present). Of the Eucharist he wrote and preached much and often. What it meant to him can be glimpsed in such extracts as the following:

> The Eucharist is the supreme way in which the people of Christ are, through our great high priest, with God with the world around on their hearts.[29]

> The author and the agent in the Eucharist is the Word of God. The Word is proclaimed in the scripture lections and in the preaching. The the same Word, who is Jesus, blesses the loaf and the cup, and invites and commands us.[30]

And the meaning of all life is here set forth, since men exist to worship God for God's own sake. . . . Like the Incarnation itself, the Eucharist is the breaking into history of something eternal, beyond history, inapprehensible in terms of history alone.[31]

For the supreme question is not what we make of the Eucharist but what the Eucharist is making of us, as (together with the Word) it fashions us into the way of Christ.[32]

It was my privilege often to stay with Bishop Michael and Lady Ramsey in their retirement homes; it was moving to see Bishop Michael in his old age in the quiet seclusion of a small flat preparing to say Evensong with his wife and any visitors. He did this as carefully and devoutly as if he were preparing for a service of several thousand people in Canterbury Cathedral, for he was just as surely 'entering into the courts of the Lord'.

With the humility of a great and godly man, Bishop Michael lived with a great sense of penitence, which often seems old-fashioned nowadays. He had an awareness that all sin, whether individual or corporate, is an offence against the love and goodness of God. A shadow would pass across his face as he spoke of it. Whenever I went to stay he would say to me on the telephone, 'I am glad you are coming, I want to talk to you about something.' I expected it to be a different subject each time, but the last three times it was the same: 'Why don't people go to confession now? Are our clergy being properly trained to hear confessions?'

In retreats and in charges to ordinands and clergy he spoke often about the meaning and value of sacramental confession and its being a vital part of our Anglican heritage. In *The Future of the Christian Church*, which he wrote in co-operation with his friend Cardinal Suenens, he had written:

. . . as absolver the priest shares, on the one hand, in the broken heart of sin and penitence, and on the other hand, in the sorrow and joy of Christ who bears our sins and pardons them.[33]

The last time I saw Bishop Michael was in Oxford when I was beginning the little anthology taken from his spiritual writings, entitled *Gateway to God*.[34] It gave him much pleasure whilst I was working on it, and appeared in the bookshops just five days before he slipped quietly through his own gateway to God. I asked him what he would most like me to include. After one of his fruitful silences he replied, 'Tell them about heaven! Tell them about heaven! That's where we are going; that is what we were created for. Heaven is the meaning of our life here. Tell them about heaven.' As he spoke there was a light in his eyes and an expression of glory on his face, such as I had seen many times when he celebrated the Eucharist. So I made the Christian hope, the hope of heaven, the first topic in *Gateway to God*, for it was the hope that had inspired his whole Christian pilgrimage, not only his old age.

In his last years Bishop Michael had to endure failing eyesight, failing health and loss of mobility. Some words of counsel addressed to another seem to have an autobiographical ring about them:

After immense activity one passes into a phase where passivity is the only way. I pray that you may be finding this passivity as the way in which the soul serves God, not by doing this or that but by passively receiving the great stream of his love and compassion.

One of Bishop Michael's best-loved saints was the Venerable Bede. In a broadcast address from the site of Bede's monastery at Jarrow to commemorate the 1300th anniversary of his birth in 673, he said of Bede, 'he prayed and he prayed and he prayed; and he read and he read and he read; and he wrote and he wrote and he wrote.' In thus describing the contribution of Bede to English Christianity he might have been giving us a self-portrait. I do not think it fanciful to suggest that he made a favourite prayer of Bede's his own, or that his prayer has been granted.

And I pray thee, merciful Jesus, that as thou hast graciously granted me to drink sweetly from the Word which tells of Thee, so wilt Thou of Thy goodness, grant that I may come at length to Thee, the fount of all wisdom, and stand before Thy face forever.

NOTES

1. *The Gospel and the Catholic Church*, Longmans, 1936.
2. Gordon S. Wakefield, 'Michael Ramsey: A Theological Appraisal', *Theology*, November 1988, p. 456.
3. Xavier Léon-Dufour SJ, *The Gospels and the Jesus of History*, Collins, 1968.
4. Owen Chadwick, *Michael Ramsey: A Life*, Clarendon Press, Oxford, 1990.
5. *The Resurrection of Christ*, Geoffrey Bles, 1945. Revised edition, Fontana 1961, p. 7.
6. *The Gospel and the Catholic Church*, op. cit., p. 6.
7. *Jesus and the Living Past*, Oxford University Press, 1980, p. 33.
8. *The Gospel and the Catholic Church*, op. cit., pp. 222–3.
9. E. Hoskyns, *Cambridge Sermons*, SPCK, 1938, p. 70.
10. *The Glory of God and the Transfiguration of Christ*, Longmans, 1949.
11. Ibid., p. 22.
12. Ibid., p. 144, 147.
13. *Theology*, op. cit., p. 456.
14. *From Gore to Temple*, Longmans, 1960.
15. Ibid., p. 162.
16. *Canterbury Pilgrim*, SPCK, 1974, p. 15.
17. *The Christian Priest Today*, SPCK, Revised Edition, 1985, p. 56.
18. This paragraph incorporates material used in my *Waymarks in the English Religious Tradition*, Fairacres Publication 91, p. 16.
19. *Lent with St John*, SPCK, 1980, p. 25.
20. *Prayers and Meditations of St Anselm, with the Proslogion*, translated by Sr Benedicta Ward SLG, Penguin Classics, 1986, p. 244.
21. *Canterbury Pilgrim*, op. cit., pp. ix, 4. (Also quoted by Eric James in *A Life of Bishop John A.T. Robinson*, Collins, 1987. p. 123).
22. *Sacred and Secular*, The Holland Lectures for 1964, Longmans, 1965, p. 45.
23. Eric James, *A Life of Bishop John A.T. Robinson*, op cit., 1987, p. 168.
24. *Be Still and Know*, Collins Fount, 1982, Preface.
25. Ibid., pp. 73–4.
26. *Holy Spirit*, SPCK, 1977, p. 131.
27. *Be Still and Know*, op. cit., p. 74.
28. *Canterbury Pilgrim*, op. cit., p. 97.
29. *The Christian Priest Today*, op. cit., p. 16.
30. *Canterbury Pilgrim*, op. cit., p. 62.
31. *The Gospel and the Catholic Church*, op. cit., pp. 119, 107.
32. *Durham Essays and Addresses*, SPCK, 1957, p. 21.
33. *The Future of the Christian Church*, SCM Press, 1971, p. 36.
34. *Gateway to God*, Darton, Longman and Todd, 1988.

Also by Lorna Kendall

Waymarks in the English Religious Tradition by Lorna Kendall. SLG Press 1984 (Fairacres Publication 91). 50 pence.

In 1984 the International Ecumenical Fellowship held its 17th International Conference, entitled 'The Pilgrim's Way', at Canterbury. Christians from many countries and different denominations gathered to worship together, to get to know each other and to share experiences of Christian pilgrimage from different traditions and cultural settings.

A unifying feature of the Conference was the daily short meditation on some aspect of the English spiritual tradition given by Dr Lorna Kendall. The meditations, which we publish here, comprise simple introductions to five people whose lives and writings stand as waymarks to guide and encourage their fellow pilgrims: the Venerable Bede, Julian of Norwich, Richard Hooker, John Bunyan and, in our own time, Archbishop Michael Ramsey of Canterbury.

Also by Michael Ramsey

The Christian Concept of Sacrifice by Michael Ramsey. SLG Press 1974 (Fairacres Publication 39). 30 pence.

At the Last Supper Jesus is recorded as saying, 'This is my blood of the Covenant.' He was explaining the meaning of his own death by using the imagery of Jewish sacrifice. What meaning was he assigning to the language? Why did the early Christian Church use this same imagery to describe the person and work of Jesus? And in the twentieth century, what does the Christian Church ascribe to this same language?

In a paper read to the Anselm Society, Michael Ramsey explores this central Christian doctrine and the theological significance of sacrifical imagery to Christian thought and worship.